IMAGES
of England

PEOPLE OF
DIDCOT

Didcot Market Place which was on The Broadway at the back of Station Road. This picture is thought to date from the 1950s, a time when rationing was a close memory and 'Home Produce' was still an important part of daily living. This photograph is reproduced by kind permission of Oxford County Council Photographic Archive.

IMAGES
of England

PEOPLE OF
DIDCOT

Compiled by
Kenneth Caulkett

TEMPUS

Tempus Publishing Limited
The Mill, Brimscombe Port,
Stroud, Gloucestershire, GL5 2QG

ISBN 0 7524 2059 3

Typesetting and origination by
Tempus Publishing Limited
Printed in Great Britain by
Midway Clark Printing, Wiltshire

This book is dedicated to Dr Victoria Hamilton BMBCh Oxon 1976, MRCP, MRCGP, DFFP, GP and to Mr Watt Smith MBBS, BDS, FDSRCS, MD and his team at the John Radcliffe Hospital, Oxford, who with their skill and hard work enabled me to complete this book.

The demolition of an old farm house on Jackson's Corner, on the junction of Foxhall Road and Broadway. The farm was originally the home of Mr and Mrs George Bowering who installed a few petrol pumps in 1931. The buildings at the rear of the farm belonged to Mr Nolder Townsend's coalyard. The photograph is reproduced by kind permission of Oxfordshire County Council Photographic Archive.

Contents

Acknowledgements

My sincere thanks to the people of Didcot who have shown much kindness to me by loaning their treasured old photographs. My sincere thanks also go to Miss Sharon Wharton for the hours of hard work on the computer and lastly to the people who made this book possible. The photographers – Mr Alfred Carpenter (permission for reproduction kindly given by his son Mr Chris Carpenter), Studio Atlanta (permission for reproduction kindly given by Don Osbourne). A special thanks also to Oxfordshire County Council Photographic Archive.

A class from Greenmere School in 1940.

Introduction

When I first started this book, some eighteen years ago, it was mainly for selfish reasons. For the wonderful childhood that I shared, with my many friends. Hard, yes, but for the most part, happy and adventurous. I was born in my grandmother's house in St Mary's Street, Wallingford, and my parents moved to Tavistock Avenue some two months later in 1938, and that was where I remained for the next fifteen years. on the Vesta Estate, made to form a square, of South Park Avenue, Bowness Avenue, Tavistock Avenue and Parkside (now Queensway). Eight houses made up Downs Road which jutted out of South Park Avenue towards the fields. A total of 199 houses were built between the years 1933 and 1936 and the residents were made up of people from all parts of Great Britain and what wonderful stories of hard times and good times and friendship would be passed on to children and grandchildren everywhere. Kynaston Road, Wessex Road and the Broadway houses were already built and the people well established within the town. Oxford Crescent Estate was now ready for residents. It was not unusual at this time for one's neighbour to be on your estate one day, and the whole family moved to a different one overnight. The houses were very full. The building of these estates was the start of the expansion of Didcot town. During the 1940s and '50s it seemed that everyone knew one another. A trip to town was a pleasure, even on an early Tappins bus, with wooden seats.

There was enough shops for the community at that time and one could well do without supermarkets. In my opinion these were Didcot's best times. But time marches on, it is only with sadness, we see the passing of our green fields, corn field, hedgerows, woodlands, streams and footpaths.

Didcot's population is increasing rapidly, and the demand for homes is incessant. Now perhaps, with the new part of the town to be built in the near future, Didcot can again become a great town with a very close and friendly community. All proceeds of this book are going to what I believe to be a worthy cause: 'The Didcot Boys' Football Club.

I have today learned, with deep regret of the passing of Mrs Rhoda Sanderson. All who attended the Barn church or club during the 1940s and '50s will remember all the voluntary hours of hard work and assistance she gave to all concerned. And I am sure she knew how grateful we all were.

I hope this book will give pleasure to all its readers, old and young, bringing back memories of all the good times enjoyed in these photographs.

Mistakes on names and spellings, I can only apologize for, as copies of photographs have been passed through pubs, clubs, cafes, friends and family, to gain as much information for the reader as possible.

To me it is my Didcot family album. Whether it brings laughter or tears, please enjoy.

K.J. Caulkett
March 2000

The Royal Oak dart team, winners of the Morelands league, 1957/58/59. Left to right, back row: Len Dunn, Alec Oats, Ken Knott, John Burton. Front row: Owen Duffy, Morny Brown, Fred Dawson, Eric Poole.

One
The Barn

The seventeenth-century tithe barn, situated on the corner of Park Road and Parkside (now Queensway). For hundreds of people of Didcot, the Barn will hold treasured memories.

The Revd Pat Keating and Leonard Burton (left) are seen outside the vestry doors of the Barn church.

A letter from Pat Keating describing the heyday of The Barn.

THE BARN :- HOW IT ALL BEGAN

In 1938 it was a 300 year old tithe Barn, part of Allen's farm, in the parish of Hagbourne.
The Oxford diocese spent one thousand pounds converting it into a mission church to serve the new housing estate known as The Vestas.
It was furnished by parishoners of All Saints Church, Didcot.

In October 1939 the then Bishop of Oxford appointed me priest - in - charge of St Peter's, Northbourne.
He wrote, " At a later date I may require you to take charge of a detached portion of the parish of Hagbourne ".
Thus the Barn passed into my charge, and I immediately had the Bishop's consent to it being run both as a church and as a social centre.

At that time the Barn was in use as a clearing - station for evacuees from London, to help with who's entertainment Lady Glyn (W . R . V . S) gave a grand piano; the long shed in the grounds was a mortuary; next door was a children's nursery with Miss Weiss as Warden.
A heavy metal screen cut off the sanctuary, used on Sunday's for Holy Communion, Evenings & occasionally on week - days also.

Thus the scene was set for one of the most exciting developments in the social life of Didcot.
The nucleus of the very first mixed club in Berkshire was already formed in the old Northbourne Vicarage; in the Barn there was the beginning of a girls club.
Before long the two combined & so became the Barn Mixed Club, with a limited membership of 100, followed in the days ahead by clubs for old time & folk dancing, boxing, ' old folks ', football teams, summer camps & the rest.
These saw almost a generation of youngsters through the difficult war years, & brought into company & friendship some of the finest young men & women it has been my privilege to know & serve.
The adults who came to serve & who stayed to worship, are for even in my heart & memory.

Pat Keating

Dear Kenneth
I am sorry that you have had to wait so long to hear from me regarding the events centred round the Barn Church during the years of 1934 - 1950.

However, I have at last managed to find what photos I have relating to the Barn and its activities at least from the year of 1947 to 1957 which was the period that I worked there under Pat Keating and Stanley Griffiths, who was as you know were the Incumbants of the parish of Northbourne, in which the Barn Church was situated.

I was known as the Lay Evanglist of the parish, which some may call as being a Stipendary Lay Reader of the parish.
My main duties were in conducting the Sunday School. where many of the children came from the Vestas Estate, and taking the Sunday evening service.
On the weekdays I was responsible for helping with large mixed youth club. which Pat Keating ran, and running Junior and Intermediate clubs for Boys and Girls.
I was responsible for raising a lot of money for the upkeep of the Barn, and paying my salary, besides being responsible for keeping the building clean and tidy and doing any repairs.

I did quite a bit of visiting in the Barn area and took a party of the youth club for a weeks holiday to Kessingland.
A photo of this party is enclosed with the rest of the photos.

In 1951 the Barn celebrated its 10th anniversary, when many special events were arranged both amongst the church folk and the clubs.

On of the major events which I took part in, arranging and carrying out was, the re - roofing of the Barn early nineteen fifties, because of the poor state of the tiles which let in a lot of water and draughts.

It proved to be a very interesting event. in the fact that nearly all those who came and volunteered to help me do the work, were young people of the Barn area of both Boys and Girls.
The only sad thing about this undertaking was having to destroy many birds nests, we could have waited and often did.
But to have to keep waiting, when coming across these nests, would have meant losing a lot of helpers, and often got a downpour of rain, when a lot of tiles were off the roof.

I hope this gives you some idea of my activities, concerning the Barn and its people.
With All Good Wishes
Leonard B Burton

Leonard Burton describing his activities at the Barn.

On Sundays and occasionally on weekdays the metal screens on the church would be removed and the sanctuary could be viewed. A general translation of the Latin inscription is: 'Where two or three are gathered together, I will be there amongst them'.

It was a sad day for all the people of Didcot when, in 1971, the Barn was destroyed deliberately by fire. It was never rebuilt. This picture shows the derelict shell of this, once thriving, church.

The first wedding to take place in the Barn was between Miss Emily Major and Mr J. Kerry in 1941. Other present included, left to right: Mr Harry Major, Frieda Major, Mrs Rose Reemer, Rhoda Major, Mr E.J. Fould, Mrs Kerry, Mr Jennings, Mrs Major, Mr J. Kerry, Mrs Emily Kerry (*née* Major), Revd Keating, Frieda Major, Jack Turner, -?-, Mr F. Major.

Younger members of the church congregation are seen outside the south wall of the barn in 1946 or 47. Among those present were: John Slade, Christine Sanderson, Jean Target, Len Burton, Pete Sanderson, John Wilcox, Tony Maynard, Margaret Swansea, Marina Birmingham, Ian Richards, Jennifer Gibbs, Julie Hopkins, Barbara Peisley, Tony Woodman, Basil Breeze, Ken Caulkett, June Young.

The congregation were often photographed outside the south wall and the some of the youngest are seen here in 1948/49. Among them are: Barbara Caulkett, Jenny Goodenough, Maureen Coles, Jackie Taylor, Dorreen Goodenough, Len Burton.

The Barn Junior Boys' Club, at Brockenhurst in 1948. Trips to the seaside were quite regular events and the beach huts seen behind this group were a regular feature in coastal town in this era; sadly few remain. Left to right, back row: -?-, ? Roper, Roy Barnard, Pete Burke, Dave Burfitt, -?-, Arthur Hitchcock. Second row from the back: Len Burton, -?-, Ray Collins, Alan Caulkett, -?-, Don Woodman. Third row: Nobby Brown, Freddy Jepson, Brian Robertson, Barry Rickard, Brian Thorhill, -?-, Bob Hopkins, Dennis Kaye, Alf Talbot, Wyndham Hopkins, Glyn Evans, Pat Keating. Front row: -?-, the daughter of Revd Keating, Pete Dawson, Pete Sanderson, Terry Brookes, Tommy Jepson, George Stewart, -?-, John Pratt, Dave Coles.

The Barn's mixed club holiday in the 1940s. The bear in the centre appears to be very docile or, more probably, a person dressed up in a costume, and was a regular feature on this holiday camp on the Isle of Wight. Left to right, back row: Alan Clair, Eric Stovin, Dennis Kaye, Tommy Tucker. Middle row: John Peisley, Christine Sanderson, bear, Dawcus Westbrook, -?-. Front row: Shirly Rickard, Arthur Hitchcock, Joan Mulford.

The Barn's mixed club holiday, Brockenhurst, 1947/8. Left to right, back row: Peter Hopkins, Gerald Collins. Middle row: Arthur Hitchcock, Gwen Collins, Mrs Sanderson, Barbara Denwood, Pearl Cobb. Front row: John Sweetser, Pam West, Beryl Cobb, Don Woodward, Len Burton, Will Kent.

Barn mixed club at Avon Tyrrell, 1949/50. These trips also included sport and leisure activities. Left to right, back row: Len Burton, Maureen Hitchmam, George Wooton, Cherry Greenough. Middle row: Arthur Hitchcock, Pete Sanderson, M. Manning, Eric Rees, Terry Brookes. Front row: Sadie Shaw, Pam Hodder, Russell Davis, Geoff Rickard.

The Barn Youth Club holiday at Kesingland in Suffolk in 1950/51. The 1950s fashion for turned-up jeans and white pumps is well in evidence. Left to right, back row: Ron Freeborn, Tony Jefferies, Len Burton, Mick Jefferies, John Wilcox. Front row: Marina Birmingham, -?-, Dawn Pilling, Audrey White.

The Barn Youth Club holiday at Peacehaven. Left to right: Gwen Collins, Eva Carter, Phyllis Lothain, Sheila Essex, Pat Watts, Nonnie Rees.

The Barn 'Over 60s' party in 1949. The participants are photographed in the grounds of the Barn, on its south side. Park Road can be seen in the background.

The Bishop of Oxford, Dr Kirk, prepares to cut the cake on the 10th anniversary of the Barn Church in 1949. Excited children look on.

Before the cutting of the cake Len Burton blew out the candles. To the right, the Revd Keating is seen enjoying the day.

A Barn choir in the 1950s. Only some of the names are known. Left to right, back row: Mr Hedges, Mrs Sanderson, Revd Keating, Len Burton, ? Thomas. Among those in the middle row: Mary Bird, Vincent Essex, Linda Price, Mavis Buckle, Martin Essex, Neville Moss. Among those in the front row: Mick Tyrrell, Bob Evans, Allan Barns, Allan Buckle, John Barnes, Tony Richens.

A Canadian party held by the Barn Young Wives Club in the 1960s. Note the old steel radiator (centre left) and next to it the grand piano, acting as an impromptu work surface. Left to right, on the left side of the table: Gloria Onions, Elizabeth ?, Pat Roberts, Pat Kent, Eileen Greenough, Pat Wiercinski, Myrtle Ashwin, Laura Cox, -?-, -?-, Eileen Mandryk, Beryl Evans, -?-, -?-. At the far end of the table: Mrs Marsh. On the right side of the table, right to left: -?-, -?-, Joyce Lubbuck, Vera Holt, Marion Johnson, -?-, -?-, Frieda Pattinson, Violet Wells, -?-, -?-, Edna Vaal, Doreen Phillips, Marjorie Holt.

An Easter party organized for the Young Wives' Club and their children. Among those sitting at the table are: Alan Martin, John Kent, Terry Jones, Nicholas Wiercinski, Elizabeth Ashwin.

Another Barn children's party, this time set at large tables. Note the mixture of old pew chairs (one marked with the owner's name), and the new chairs.

A children's party in 1953/54. In the centre Graham Mitchell is seen joking with his brother, Steve, and missing the photograph.

The prize giving for the Barn Table Tennis Club in the 1950s. Brigadier Weir is seen congratulating Geoff Rickard, with the Revd Keating standing to the right. Sat down behind the Brigadier and Geoff is Percy Ball and sat to their right are Barbara Dorling and Zena Ackerman.

Members of the Barn Table Tennis Club enjoying a cup of tea in the early 1950s. Left to right, back row: -?-, Jeanette McDonald, Arthur Frost, Jim Willis, Robin Walters, Brian Slade, Jimmy Marshall, Joe Willis. Front row: Barbara Peisley, Cherry Greenough, Bob Pullen, George Pullen, Bob Willis, Eddie Willis, Shirley Burton, Robin Burton.

The Table Tennis Club in 1955. Left to right, standing: -?-, Eddie Willis, Gerald Collins, Pete Thompson, James Willis, Ray Carter, Bob Willis. Seated: George Pullin, Robin Burton, Ronie Brown, Barbara Peisley, John Peisley, Arthur Frost.

Physical training at the Barn in the 1950s. The photograph was taken outside the old mortuary which had been disused, as a mortuary, since the late 1940s. The main use from this date on seems to have been as a venue for the Table Tennis Club. At the top is: Brian Wells. Left to right, second row down: Pat Wear, Reg Stokoe. Third row: Brian Bidmead, Robin Morgan, Keith Evans. Bottom row: John Callaghan, Sam Essex, Eddie Willis, 'Basher' Birmingham.

The physical training team on show in the vicarage gardens in 1950s. Left to right: Eddie Willis, John Callaghan, 'Basher' Birmingham, Reg Stokoe, Brian Wells, Sam Essex, Robin Morgan, Pat Wear, Keith Evans, Brian Bidmead. Robert 'Snowy' Newton can be seen in the background standing behind the horse and Brian Wells.

23

A Barn church fancy dress competition in 1950. A group event, this tableau depicting a priest and the wedding party won first prize. Left to right, they are: Tony Kitchener, Muriel Till, Doreen Milne, Janet Vincent, Jackie Turner.

The Barn was ideally situated at the Southwest corner of Edmonds Park. During the summer most sports, games and pastimes were played here. On this occasion Mr Carpenter photographed a low flying Sterling Four Engine Bomber. This type of aircraft was often used to tow two gliders at a time and frequently took off from the Chiltern-Harwell airbase.

Two
People and Places

A Lagonda motorcar and a pintsized version outside the Queen's public house in 1920. Arch Napper is seen in the jodhpurs and flat cap to the left and the landlord of the pub, Sid Napper, is seen to the right. The young boy in front is John Napper.

Dales shop on the High Street in 1920. Dales sold most items including hardware, clothes and foods. Seen here are Mrs Downing (*née* Butler) on the left and Betty Green on the right. The shop finally closed down in the 1970s.

Ladies outside Didcot's old gasworks in 1916. Left to right: Myra Butler, Iris Dowding, Amy Seward, -?-, Bessie Green.

Founder members of the Marlborough Club. The club is still in operation and now has 900 members. Only some of the members seen are known. First right, back row is Daniel Lyford, son of Jimmy. Third from the right, back row is Mr Tugwell. On the front row, centre is Mr Tugwell and to the right of him is Mr Simmonds.

Workmen involved in the building of the officers' mess, Vauxhall Barracks, 1938. Third from the left is Jim Smith.

Didcot post office, at the top of Station Road, in the 1920s. At this time it was run by Mr and Mrs Richardson, who later retired to Hagbourne.

Didcot's Silver Band in the 1930s. Fourth from the right in the back row is Bert Giles and in the centre of the middle row is Mr Bellamy (bandmaster). On the far right of the middle row is Mr W. 'Dick' Nunn.

From left to right: George, Joy and Jane Walton and a young friend, Valerie Rickard, in 1945. This picture shows the route to school taken by the children, across ploughed fields. Greenmere and St Birinus are just visible behind the children's heads. The holiday farm, now long gone, would have been to the right, near the railway bridge – on the Didcot to Newbury line.

Some of the Vesta children who walked the path across the fields to school. They are seen here in 1945.

8th June, 1946

TO-DAY, AS WE CELEBRATE VICTORY, I send this personal message to you and all other boys and girls at school. For you have shared in the hardships and dangers of a total war and you have shared no less in the triumph of the Allied Nations.

I know you will always feel proud to belong to a country which was capable of such supreme effort; proud, too, of parents and elder brothers and sisters who by their courage, endurance and enterprise brought victory. May these qualities be yours as you grow up and join in the common effort to establish among the nations of the world unity and peace.

George R.I

A copy of the letter sent out in 1946 to schoolchildren to commemorate the end of the Second World War.

IMPORTANT WAR DATES

1939
SEP 1. Germany invaded Poland
SEP 3. Great Britain and France declared war on Germany; the B.E.F. began to leave for France
DEC 13. Battle of the River Plate

1940
APR 9. Germany invaded Denmark and Norway
MAY 10. Germany invaded the Low Countries
JUNE 3. Evacuation from Dunkirk completed
JUNE 8. British troops evacuated from Norway
JUNE 11. Italy declared war on Great Britain
JUNE 22. France capitulated
JUNE 29. Germans occupied the Channel Isles
AUG 8–OCT 31. German air offensive against Great Britain (Battle of Britain)
OCT 28. Italy invaded Greece
NOV 11–12. Successful attack on the Italian Fleet in Taranto Harbour.
DEC 9–11. Italian invasion of Egypt defeated at the battle of Sidi Barrani

1941
MAR 11. Lease-Lend Bill passed in U.S.A.
MAR 28. Battle of Cape Matapan
APR 6. Germany invaded Greece
APR 12–DEC 9. The Siege of Tobruk
MAY 20. Formal surrender of remnants of Italian Army in Abyssinia
MAY 20–31. Battle of Crete
MAY 27. German battleship *Bismarck* sunk
JUNE 22. Germany invaded Russia
AUG 12. Terms of the Atlantic Charter agreed
NOV 18. British offensive launched in the Western Desert
DEC 7. Japanese attacked Pearl Harbour
DEC 8. Great Britain and United States of America declared war on Japan

1942
FEB 15. Fall of Singapore
APR 16. George Cross awarded to Malta
OCT 23–NOV 4. German-Italian army defeated at El Alamein
NOV 8. British and American forces landed in North Africa

1943
JAN 31. The remnants of the 6th German Army surrendered at Stalingrad
MAY Final victory over the U-Boats in the Atlantic
MAY 13. Axis forces in Tunisia surrendered
JULY 10. Allies invaded Sicily
SEP 3. Allies invaded Italy
SEP 8. Italy capitulated
DEC 26. *Scharnhorst* sunk off North Cape

1944
JAN 22. Allied troops landed at Anzio
JUNE 4. Rome captured
JUNE 6. Allies landed in Normandy
JUNE 13. Flying-bomb (V.1) attack on Britain started
JUNE Defeat of Japanese invasion of India
AUG 25. Paris liberated
SEP 3. Brussels liberated
SEP 8. The first rocket-bomb (V.2) fell on England.
SEP 17–26. The Battle of Arnhem
OCT 20. The Americans re-landed in the Philippines

1945
JAN 17. Warsaw liberated
MAR 20. British recaptured Mandalay
MAR 23. British crossed the Rhine
APR 25. Opening of Conference of United Nations at San Francisco
MAY 2. German forces in Italy surrendered
MAY 3. Rangoon recaptured
MAY 5. All the German forces in Holland, N.W. Germany and Denmark surrendered unconditionally
MAY 9. Unconditional surrender of Germany to the Allies ratified in Berlin
JUNE 10. Australian troops landed in Borneo
AUG 6. First atomic bomb dropped on Hiroshima
AUG 8. Russia declared war on Japan
AUG 9. Second atomic bomb dropped on Nagasaki
AUG 14. The Emperor of Japan broadcast the unconditional surrender of his country
SEP 5. British forces re-entered Singapore

MY FAMILY'S WAR RECORD

A VE day street party on South Park Avenue on the Vesta Estate in 1945. Among those present were: Mrs Watson, Mrs Rees, Mr Grimes, Mrs Peisley, Randall Rees, Roy Barnard, George Stewart, Paddy Watson, Gerald Hunt, Barbara Peisley, Neville Waddicor.

Another VE day street party on Parkside (now Queensway) on the Vesta Estate.

VE day being celebrated on Oxford Crescent in 1945. Among the people at the party were: Kenny Mills, Frieda Sayers, Brian Mills, Tony Mayner, Robert Treadwell, Margaret Wilson, Yvonne Turner.

VE day fancy dress party on Oxford Crescent in 1945. At the party were: Mia Lloyd, Dawny Lloyd, Yvonne Turner, Jackie Turner, Anita Turner, Reg Studley, Richard Studley, Margaret Goldworthy, Rosemary Harris, John Hodston, Carol Trinder. Yvonne Turner, as Winston Churchill, won the fancy dress competition.

Preparations for VJ night, 4 August 1945. The photograph, taken by Mr George 'Yorky' Walton, shows Vesta Estate residents stood on and around the part-built bonfire in South Park Avenue. Some of those seen in the photograph are: Don Woodward, Bob Escot, Nobby Brown, Pete Haydon, Pete Burke, Ray Hancock, Ron Escot, Bob Kaye, Randall Rees, Roy Barnard (evacuee) Louis Haydon, Nonnie Rees, Gerald Hunt, Don Robertson, Gracie Stewart, Barry Rickard, Tommy Jepson, Phillip Haydon, Bob Hopkins, Harold Bennett.

The Americans gave a party for local children in Edmonds Park at the end of the war in 1945. Two members are seen here ceremonially folding their national flag, the Stars and Stripes.

Miss Brenda Jepson seen at the celebrations for VJ day in Edmonds Park. Note the trellis tables to the left and the car on the right.

Barry Rickard (left) and Ken Caulkett (right) on a home-made trolley on Tavistock Avenue in 1947.

The first bananas in Didcot after the Second World War were delivered to Fred Nobbs shop in Park Road, a site now occupied by ATS Tyres. Among those seen here are: Dave Coles (a young boy caught on camera 'playing hooky' from school), Dorothy Snow, Mrs Wrathall, Fred Nobbs, Mr Nobbs Snr. The small children and the baby in the pram are unknown.

Parties at the Didcot Community Centre. This was situated behind the then White Hart public house, now Broadways, at the top of Station Road. Many clubs and societies used these premises.

Gladys Nobbs on her new trade bike in 1939.

Cadets march past in the British Legion fête and parade in 1948. Maureen Peppin is accompanying the cadets on a bicycle and among the cadets are: Maurice Wicks, Neil Robertson, John Cummings, John Watson.

The Barn theatre club in the 1950s. Left to right, back row: Audrey Cresswell, -?-, Ellen Blackmore, Windy Brind, Betty Dawson, Bill Brind. Front row: Arthur Hitchcock, Eva Blackmore, Phyllis Kingham, -?-, Mrs Holliday, -?-, Dudley Butcher.

Alan Caulkett (left) relaxing with friends Barry Rickard and Freddy Jepson on a Sunday afternoon in Edmonds Park, 1954. Cricket and football were played on the fields here at this time. Note part of the old canning factory and the flats on Newland Avenue in the background. Both have now gone.

Left to right: Mrs Hodston, Mrs Kitchener and Mrs Daw are seen outside the shops on Wantage Road. The Baptist church can be seen in the background. To the left a battery powered wheelchair is ready for the off.

Tony Kitchener is seen receiving a plaque from Mrs Cullen at Manor School sports day in June 1950. Others present are: Sheila Cummings, Mrs Turner, Mrs Knight, Eileen Embleton, Mrs Harris, Susan Knight, Barbara Harris.

A group of friends in 1946. Left to right, back row: Myra Lloyd, -?-, Moll Oaks, Beryl Reeves. Front row: Doris Stratton, Evelyn Pearce, Betty Oaks.

A fancy dress event in the 1950s. Fancy dress and pram races around local public houses, to raise money for charity. Much effort went into these events as can be seen.

Christmas at the Vauxhall Youth Club in 1955. This club was situated at the Camp, near the old Civvy Club, along North Road. Among the group are: Rosemary Pitt, Nessie Chalton, Beryl Statter, Maureen Coutch, ? Smith, Stewart Rose.

Waiting to see the Queen who was on her way to visit the Atomic Research Laboratory at Harwell in 1955. The onlookers include: Andrew Saunders, Peter Crossingham, Graham Sainders, Mrs Gwen Saunders (with her daughter Brienne), Doreen Howlett, Mrs Howlett, Sheila Howlett.

Party time at the Royal Oak public house in 1950. Left to right, in the foreground, are: Morny Brown, John Litton, Tom Waddicor, Nobby Brown, Don Woodwood, John Sweetser.

A club photograph in 1950. Malcolm Thornhill is standing at the back. The rest are, left to right: Gordon Bailey, Amy Wigley, Pete Gregory, Pam Smith, Arthur Frost, Florries Wigley, Eric Smith.

These stylish young men enjoy a pint before the dance. They are, left to right: Dave 'Bonk' Coles, Freddy Jepson, Brian 'Blogsy' Roberton, Brian 'Bosel' Bosley, Alfie Barham, Barry Rickard.

Left to right: Alec Oats, John Burton, Morny Brown, -?-, John Dobson, Dennis Sage, Dick Oxley waiting for the dance.

The Civilian Club, Vauxhall Barracks, in the 1950s. Left to right, standing: 'Paddy' ?, a corporal in the Army Catering Corps, Billy Bray, Phil Hemmings, -?-, Trevor Bray, -?-, Billy Mitchell, Lofty Dentor. Seated: Loft Wright, Mr Burgoyne, Dick Nunn, Mr Robinson.

The coronet ballroom in 1954.

Participants at an old-time dancing party.

Members of Didcot Cycle Speedway team, which began in 1951. Left to right, back row: Freddy Jepson, Neil Robertson, Gerald Hunt, Johnny Watson, Dave Coles, Tommy Jepson, Ray Collings. Standing in front of the team members are Kathy and Margaret Warwick.

Senior and junior members of the Didcot Meteors Cycle Speedway team in 1951. Left to right, they are: John Christopher, Dave Coles, Freddy Jepson, Dave Burfitt, Paddy Watson, Brian Robertson, David Seymour, Dave Cullen, Dave Kent.

Didcot motorcycle club in the 1950s. Members on the club included Bob Willis, Gerald Collings, Eddie Willis, June Vincent, John Breed, Joan Gregory, Yorky Walton.

Windy Corner at Thruxton on 28 March 1951. Eddie Willis is seen here in his first race, in which he came fifth, winning two pounds and ten shillings. Eddie raced competitively for five years.

Didcot 'People of Cycles' tour in Newhaven, August 1949. The tour cycled 397 miles around the South East Coast starting from Bognor. The participants were, left to right: Francis Adams, George Sutton, Brian Hickman, Ron 'Twink' Sears, Harold Coles, Amy Wigley, Reg Dodds, Fred Ritson, Tony White. Francis Adams (first left) started the photography shop, Studio Atlanta in 1939/40. She later emigrated to Canada when Mr Harold Coles (centre) took over the business.

Didcot community centre's cycle ride in 1949. They took a cycle ride of 58 miles. Among others are: Harold Coles, Ron 'Twink' Sears, Amy Wigley, Florrie Wigley, George Sutton, Fred Ritson, Frank Hill, Terry Mole, Reg Dads, Brian Hickman, Witty ?.

The Carnival Queen and runners up in 1960. The Queen was Pauline Edwards and here attendants were: Doreen Weller (left) and Valerie Kinch (right).

The Carnival Queen travelling down Station Road on British Rail road transport in the 1950s. The Queen was June Murray and her attendants were June Thornton and Margaret Morgan (?)

All Saints church youth group, 1958/9. Left to right, standing: Anita Turner, Gill Fox, Nevill Waddicor, Barbara Caulkett, Mike Newman, June Nevitt, Dave Shugar, John Shephard. Seated: Jean Caulkett, Peggy Newman.

The boys of All Saints church choir, 1951/52. Basil Breeze, Eric Smith and Brian Cobb are among those seen here.

Employees of the Dee Bee dartboard factory in 1975. The boss, Bernie Young (seen centre in the suit) was giving a party for his employees in celebration of being awarded the OBE for the Trade Abroad. Some of the people are known. Kneeling at the front are: Jane Bray, Gladys Hawkins, Daph ?, Chris Davis, Ruth Isles. Standing: Dennis Sage, John O'Meara, Christine James, Mary Stratton, Maureen ?, John Coulton, Dave Russell.

Workers of the print firm, Expdo, in 1951. The offices were situated at the east end of Wessex Road. Left to right, back row: Brian Wells, Ray Smith, Wedgi Kiffe, Mr Purfitt. Front row: Rose Hare, Florence Embleton, Anne Townsend.

Members of the Didcot Council in the 1960s. Mrs Downing is seated on the right.

Council workers taking a break in the 1960s. Left to right they are: Eric Smith, Dave Barham, John Gilbert, -?-.

An advertisement for Eric Tolley and his orchestra. As an individual musician, Eric played in a big band and, with them, won the Championship of Great Britain at The Winter Gardens in Blackpool. Other championships that they won included: Oxfordshire, held in Oxford; Wiltshire in Swindon; West of England in Bristol; and Greater London and The Midlands in Birmingham.

A dinner dance at the labour club in 1960.

Patrons outside the Sprat public house in 1960. Lucy James, Ron James, Mrs Haycroft, Gail Bennett and Jim Slade are all to be seen here.

The Studio Atlanta shop on Lower Broadway. The Studio Atlanta photography business was first started by Francis Adams in 1940 (see p. 47). When Francis later emigrated to Canada, the shop was taken over by Mr Harold Coles, also seen in previous pages, see also p. 47. The shop was then managed by Mr Ted Smith, who later emigrated to Australia. Since 1962 the business has been managed by Don Osbourne, who now lives in Drayton Village. The photograph shows Eric Smith outside his brother's shop in 1960.

A street party in Ridgeway Road in 1950. Among those on the left side of the table are: June Carter, Caroline Carter, Joy Clifton, Mrs Taylor, Joe Goodall, Joey Goddard, Mrs Yeldoen, Pat Yelden, Miss Carter, Eileen Coles, Shirley Kent, Mrs Hill, Betty Watson, Pam Ayres, Jean Parker. On the right side are: Mick Murphy, Mrs Yates, Miss Murphy, Mrs Carter, Mrs Clifton, Lesley Powell, Tony Goddard, Brian Yelden, Trevor Coles, Harold Coles, Mrs Ayres, Mick Bick, Ron Carter, Arthur Cross, Bob Hill, Dick Ayres, Edwin King, Mick Marriot, Mrs Parker, Mrs Kent.

Participants in an Abingdon Road fancy dress party, in 1951, which included Eric Smith, Tony Mayner and Roy Davis.

Arthur Napper's steam locomotive *OLDTIMER* rounds Davis Corner in the 1950s. At the Wallingford Arms crossroads, Tappins Garage is obscured by smoke.

A large crowd enjoy an afternoon of entertainment in Smallbones field in 1911. They appear to have been involved in a fancy dress football match. Note the linesman, holding a flag, on the right, and the, rather large, goal mouth that they are gathered in.

A nice peaceful Sunday on The Broadway in the 1940s. Note the elm trees lining the south side of the road. The turning to the right is St Peter's Road.

Newlands Avenue during construction in 1951. The flats at the top of the picture were nearing completion and the Italian prisoner of war camp (the arched prefabricated buildings of the left) was about to be demolished. Lynmouth Road was later to be built on the left of the picture.

Didcot's first self-service shop of The Broadway. This picture must predate 1971, as the advertisements in the window are displayed in pounds shillings and pence.

A photograph taken from the top of the New Coronet Cinema which shows what, at the time, remained of the Italian prisoner of war camp. Didcot Health Centre, the Ambulance and the Fire Station now stand in the foreground.

Mr Clargo with her baby daughter in 1920. Harry Cummings is seen holding the cow.

The district nurse, Nurse Bird, is seen here beginning her daily rounds from her home in Park Road. Mrs Bird is in the doorway. In her long career, Nurse Bird brought many babies into the world.

Collecting for Didcot Rugby Club in fancy dress in the 1960s. Left to right are: Pat Smith, Ron James, Lucy James, Mrs Fear, Mr Fear.

A cycle race in Jobs Field in 1949. The reason for the scarves covering their faces is unknown. Left to right, they are: Leyton Edwards, Frank Hill, George Sutton, Ron ?, Phil Humphries.

The mechanics taking a break at Jobs Dairy in the 1950s. Left to right, they are: Dick Valentine, Ron 'Twink' Sears, Pay Blyth, Jimmy Brown (traveller).

Didcot TA awaiting a train at the local railway station to take them on a fortnight's annual camp. Note the assortment of kit bags and luggage ... and the cheeky chappie fourth from the left.

Patrons waiting to watch *Holiday of the Buses*, the last film to be shown at the New Coronet Cinema before it closed in March 1974. The Coronet was later turned into a bingo hall which is still there. The photograph is reproduced by kind permission of Oxfordshire County Council Photographic Archive.

Three
Sports and Pastimes

A typical Saturday football game at Edmunds Park in 1949/50. Eddie Burke races to save the day.

A young Barn minors team, 1949. Left to right, back row: Derek Pryke, John Mayall, Bomber Reeves, Steve 'Saus' Freeman, George Manning, Pete Dawson. Front row: John Wilkins, Geoff Rickard, Pete Sanderson, Jim Buckle. The team's reserves were: Dave 'Bonk' Coles and Tommy Jepson.

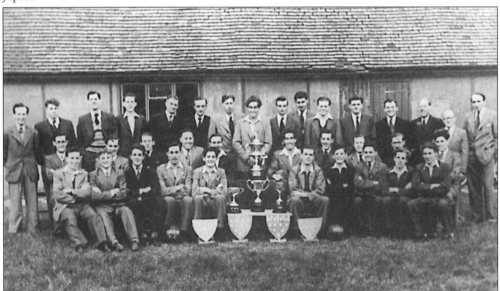

Minors and seniors of the Barn football club in 1950. Left to right, back row: Arthur Hitchcock, Tom Waddicor, Bob Escot, John Walker, Fred 'Buffy' Belcombe, Cyril Hawkins, Will Kent, Bob Willis, Don Woodward, Frank Headington, Eric Hanley, Morny Brown, Mil Brown, Mr Sanderson, Danny Shut, Revd Pat Keating. Middle row: Len Barclay, Norman Jacobs, Bill Robson, Percy Ball, Len Smith, Eddie Willis, Gerald Collins, Gwillam Evans, Sam Treehern, Don Woodman. Front row: Geoff Gickard, Derek Pryke, John Mayall, Jim Buckle, John Davis, Pete Dawson, Wyndham Hopkins, Pete Sanderson, Dave 'Bonk' Coles, John Wilkins.

The Barn's senior football club in the 1950s. Left to right, back row: Danny Shut, Gerald Collins, Ray Smith, Roy Laidlaw, John Green, Bob Escot, Sam Treehern, Ralph Ackerman. Front row: John Wilkins, Pete Dawson, Len Barclay, Eddie Burke, Don Woodward.

A six-a-side team from the Barn in the 1950s. Left to right, back row: Cyril Lovelock, Ray Young, Percy Ball. Front row: Don Woodward, Len Barclay, Doug Robertson.

A Barn team on a trip to Belgium in the 1950s. Left to right, back row: G. Gordon, Pete Dawson, Bill Duggan, Don Woodward, Roy Laidlaw, Joe Foley, Ken Knott. Front row: John Morrison, Owen Duffy, P. Henderson, T. Woods, Les Betteridge.

The Barn's senior team, also in the 1950s. Left to right, back row: Danny Shut, Morny Brown, Bill Robson, Roy Aplin, Bob Escot, Bob Willis, Don Woodward, Percy Ball, Ralph Ackerman. Front row: Eric Hanley, Len Barclay, Len Smith, Sam Treehern, Eddie Willis.

Len Barclay is seen receiving the North Berks cup for the Barn.

A Sunday morning kick-about team seen in the late 1940s. This type of kick-about in Edmonds Park usually lasted until 11.45a.m., so that the young men could reach the Royal Oak public house by 12.00 noon. Left to right, back row: Pete Bishop, Bill Saunders, Ron Stratton, Ray Butcher, John Burton, Roy 'Nobby' Brown. Front row: Morny Brown, Dicky Reece, Len Smith, John Harrison, Tom Waddicor.

An early Didcot Athletics team in the 1950s. Left to right, back row: ? Law, Nobby Brown, Ted Dadds, John Gallaghan, Fred Belcombe. Middle row: Len Franks, Fred Wigley, Reg Hooker, Ray Dicks, Arthur Bennett. Front row: Bob Thompson, George Brinton, Ron Dadds.

Many athletics teams had youth divisions and Didcot was no exception. This youth team is seen in the 1950s. The two officials were Fred 'Buffy' Belcombe (left) and Joe Alvey (right). The team included the goalkeeper Yaxley (centre) and full backs Lloyd and Briscoe. The halfbacks were Abbott, Talbot and Davis and the forwards were McCloughlin, Spindler, Hazel, Saunders and Goth.

Didcot Town Representative football match in the 1950s. Left to right, back row: Geoff Gulliver, Ted Wilkins, Don Drew, Stan Wick (Chelsea), Bomber Reeves (Reading), Cyril Fletcher (Dartford), John Fletcher. Front row: Gordon Grille, Maurice Evans (Reading), Fred Wigley, Jimmy Wheeler (Reading), John Brooks (Spurs and England).

Didcot Rovers in 1950. Left to right, back row: Norman Frazer, Windum Hopkins, John 'Mousey' Morris, -?-, Mick Ryman, Dave East, Ted Williams, -?-, Pete Burke, Fred 'Buffy' Belcombe, -?-. Front row: Mayor of Wallingford, Dave 'Bonk' Coles, Dave Burfitt, Dave Strange, Maurice Evans, Tommy 'Ginger' Reagan.

In the days of the steam train, in the 1950s, football matches were played at the town grounds on Station Road. The buildings in the background were part of the old railway staff hostel. The table tennis club later used this building.

Didcot Town football team stood in the goalmouth in the 1950s. Left to right, back row: Stan Cool, Derek Pryke, Brian Wood, Ken Rumble, John Davis, Cyril Fletcher, George Pullen, Geoff Gulliver. Front row: Ken Winter, Ted Wilkins, Don Woodward, Harry Marriot, David Burfitt, -?- (possibly a soldier from the army camp).

An earler Didcot Town football team, this time in 1930. Left to right, back row: Fred Simmonds (trainer), Pete Brown, Carlie Ruddle, Bill Cook, Midge Andrews (goalkeeper), Fred Bennett, Jack Harris, Arthur Goodall. Front row: Claude Ryman, Jack Cook, Vic Goodall, W. Britten, Fred Goodall.

Brian Doe holds the Berks and Bucks Cup aloft in the 1954/55 season. He is seen here playing for Cholsey Minors, as it was not unusual for Didcot footballers to play for local villages. Left to right, they are: Barry Rickard, Keith Mann, Maurice Arnold, Brian Doe (with cup), Dave Burfitt, John Wilson, Brian Wood, Tony Lovett, Ted Wilkins.

Harwell football team, winners of the cup, in the 1950s. Note what might be the team bus in the left background. Left to right, back row: Malcolm Mulford, Fred Lovelock, Derek Moore, Edward Ireson, George Stewart. Front row: Dave Coles, Jeff King, Arthur Bennett, Bill Connolly, Mervyn Herbert, Reg Dadds.

A young Harwell football team, 1926/27. Left to right, back row: Peter Slade, Sidney Prior, Douglas Wilson. Middle row: Reginald Prior, Leslie Elderfield, Cecil Leach, Jack Belcher, Frank Blisset. Front row: Albert Hall, Albert Leach, Jack Butler.

A Long Wittenham Reserves football team in 1950. Third from the right in the front row is Alf Greenough. The rest of the team is unknown.

The prize giving for the Didcot Boys football club in the 1960s. Fred 'Buffy' Belcombe stands on the far left.

Mr Fred 'Buffy' Belcombe receiving a certificate giving him life membership to the Didcot Boys football club on 16 June 1991. Fred has participated in the training of children and youth football teams for over fifty years.

Didcot Youth Club netball team in 1960. Left to right: Barbara Caulkett, Carol James, -?-, Patricia King, Nessie ?, Pauline Sawyer, Jill Gregory.

Didcot Youth Club netball team in 1958. Left to right, back row: Veronica Elsley, Sophia McCloughlin, Vivian Collins, Barbara Caulkett. Front row: -?-, Gillian Humphries, Margaret Ryan, -?-.

Didcot post office netball team in the 1950s. Left to right: Sophia McCloughlin, Vivienne Collins, Sheila Lawrence, Marion Hore, Joan Balsam, Christine Collins, Dorothy Wills.

The league winning Royal Oak dart team in 1957. Left to right: George Shaw, Ronnie Shaw, Joe Pope, Larry Shaw, Cyril Lovelock, Mr Buckingham (landlord), Mrs Buckingham.

Didcot Rugby team was founded by Ted Turner in September 1938. Their first game was played in the Didcot Hospital grounds and they are seen here at only their second match since their formation. The team is still going strong and red and white is still worn. Among the players seen here are: Ted Turner, Stan Lnight, Arthur Durnwell, Windsor James, Harry Casswell, Joe Davies.

The rugby team outside the Royal Oak in 1958. Note the two entrances, one marked Off Licence and one marked Private Bar. This was a usual arrangement for pubs in the days before licensed premises were allowed onto the high street. One entrance would enter into the bar area with seating, and the other entrance usually opened directly onto a high bar where you could order your bottled drinks to take away. Among the team are: Ken Knott, Brian Dowding, Jim Turner.

Didcot Rugby Club in 1969. Left to right, back row: -?-, Mick Grant, Woody ?, Clive Burnham, Ray Cox, John Potter, Jeff Boyack, Dave Hall, John Flemming. Front row: Nibry Jarvis, -?-, R. Wing, Eric Parrot, Pete Curry, Ray Manclarv.

Didcot playing Oxford RUFC for the Oxfordshire Knockout Cup in 1977. The Didcot players (in single striped kit) are, left to right: Clive Burnham, Roger Wing, Richard McGibbon, Robert Paterson, Mick Galpin, Louis Caldron. In front is Spratty Edwards.

Didcot rugby team seen outside the tennis courts at Edmonds Park in 1980. Left to right, back row: Mick Zalankas, Paul Bryan, Andy Cauldrick, Simon Beard, Ven Segesdy, Clive Burnham, Dave Hall, Mick Galpin, Richard McGibbon. Front row: Paul McCloughlin, Steve Bryan, Pete Edwards, Steve Thomas, John Dobson, Taffy Davies.

Four
Schools and Outings

The children of Manor School in the 1920s. Present were: Arthur Napper, Jack Newman, Les Smallbone, Ron Ryman, Bill Miles, Joyce Mortimer, Albert Beard, Charlie Wilcox, The Carters, The Hitchcocks, Tony Curtis, Joan Napper, Vic Goodall, Bernard Barlow, Harold Upham, Phillip Cobb, Dave Wigley, Bob Finn, Alf Burton, Malcolm Belcher.

Manor School in the 1920s.

A class from Greenmere School in the 1940s.

The football First XI at Didcot Secondary Modern Boys School, 1949. Left to right, back row: Hansford, Ryman, Fuller, Goulding, Freeman, Kent, Burnham, Town, Christopher, Mr L. Barclay. Front row: Hopkins, Mr Timewell (headmaster), Buckle, Sanderson, Brough, H.R. Williams, Wilkins.

The football First XI at Didcot Secondary Modern Boys School, 1950/51. Left to right, back row: Mr Timewell, H. Collins, P. Ashfield, A. Harris, Peter Honeyborn, S. Smith, Mr L. Barclay. Front row: D. Strange, M. Jefferies, G. Flemming, J. Broughton, Barry Rickard, B. Houghton, P. Dawson.

Didcot Secondary Modern Boys Junior XI, 1950/51. Left to right, back row: Mr J. Timewell (headmaster), T. Payne, Harry Marrit, ? Hams (goalkeeper), H.T. Strange, D. Powell, Mr G. Robinson. Front row: D. Eldridge, -?-, John Slade, Alan 'Butch' Elking (captain), John Wilcox, D. Roberts, -?-.

Didcot Secondary Modern Boys School, 1949/50. Left to right, back row: C.S. Page, J. Murrel, S. Banker, T.R. Williams, S. Rigby, Len Barclay. Front row: H.R. Williams, W.H.D. Robinson, J. Timewell (headmaster) J. Luckett, A. Nutt.

A carnival celebration at Manor School in 1950. Note the queen with her attendants sat on a dais to the left and the country dancing in the foreground.

Children entertaining at Manor School in 1950.

A Royal Oak public house outing to Southsea in 1959. Left to right, standing: San Nakervis, Morny Brown, -?-. Seated: Mrs McInnerny, Mr McInnerny, John Burton, Mrs Burton, Nobby Brown, Joan Brown (wife of Morny).

A Tappins coach trip waiting for the off in Wessex Road in the 1950s. Mrs Burton is fifth from the left.

The Rural District Council Engineering Department staff outing. Left to right: -?-, George Hunt, Tom Morse, Cyril Parsons, Freddy Jones, Joyce Dovey.

A Royal Oak trip to Brighton in 1958. Left to right: Morny Brown, Stan Nankervis, Nobby Brown, Neil Williams, Randall Rees, Joan Burton.

A trip to Butlins in the 1950s. Let to right: Dave Coles, George Stewart, Tommy Jepson, Derek Pryke, Pete 'Polly' Cleverly.

Butlins in Clacton in 1947. Left to right: Gwylum Evans, Pete Bishop, Ron Hincliffe, Nobby Brown, Bob Richardson, Buster Stovin, Dicky Rees.

A ladies day out in 1942. Among those present are: Mrs Abbott, Mrs Oaks, Mrs Casich, Mrs Hitchman, Mrs Larson, Mrs Watson, Mrs Target, Mrs Horon, Mrs Brewster, Mrs Wells, Mrs Sanderson, Mrs Littlejohn, Barbara Denwood, Pat Robson, Mrs Denwood, Mrs Saunders.

A trip to Brighton by the Didcot Community Centre in August 1948. Left to right: Roy Goodenough, Edgar Jones, Eric Randell, ? Banall, Harold Coles, Innis Gallo, Sam Essex, Fred Rouse, Fred Rixon, Maurice Elgar.

A day trip to Brighton in the 1950s. Among those present are: Bill Walpole, Maureen Ackerman, Mr and Mrs Burke, Mrs Dawson, Mr Caswell, Mrs O'Neil, Rennie Bullock, Mrs McInnerny, Roy Burke, Mary Burke, Eddie Burke, Steve O'Neil, Hazel O'Neil, Ted Turner, Sandra McInnerny, Morny Brown, Nobby Brown, Evan Rees.

A trip to Southend in the 1950s. Among those present are, at the back: ? Melgar, Gordon James, Bill Brown, Fred Rouse, Stan Gallo, Edna Cook, Frieda Barrow, Harold Coles, Jill Gregory, Barbara Whitehead, 'Nimmo'. At the front: Edgar Jones, Phillip White, Press Wells, Innis Gallo, Sam Essex, Pete Essex, Reg Town, Alan Beare, Bill Rouse, Elfyn Rouse, 'Twico'.

A rugby trip to Twickenham seen outside Tappins old garage at the end of Park Road in the 1950s. Among those present are: Cyril ?, ? McNeil, Jim O'Brien, Evan Blake, Terry McInnerny, Jack Gallagher, Tom Waddicor, Harry Caswell, Stan Nankervis, Jack Trainer, Neil Williams, Charlie Talbot, Robert McConnell, Danny Lloyd, Reg Nankervis, Fred Sawyer, Les Harding, Dai Harding, Pat Walters, Yanto Rees, Bill Caswell, Jim Turner.

Staff at Didcot Provender Stores at the Railway in 1913. Back row, fourth from the left is Fred Brown. Second row from the back, far right is Edwin Tyrell. Third row, sixth from the left is Mr Cullen.

A trip to Rhyl, Wales, in 1950. Left to right, they are: Fred Hill, Ted Humphries, George Sutton, Ron Sears.

Five
The Railways

Plate layers outside the West End signal box in 1932.

Builders on the new loco shed in Didcot in 1931/32. Bill Whiteman is seen second row from the top, on the left.

Supporters off to see a Rugby match in 1946. Left to right: H. Merrick, B. Morgan, I. Morgan, T. Morris, G. Merrick, Ray Matthews, T. Watts, Glyn Evans.

Railway men in the old days. Left to right: -?-, ? Stock, David Ireland.

The old goods shed, power house and provender stores.

The provender stores in its heyday.

The end of the provender stores in Didcot. The stores were originally built in 1885 to provide hay and food stuffs for the railway's livestock. It was finally demolished, after ninety-one years of service, in 1976.

A photograph taken from the top of the provender stores showing provender pond, with the main line and station in the background.

A LMS engine in 1955. A proud young fireman, Ken Caulkett aged seventeen (right), is seen with driver Fred ? from Oxford.

The first gas turbine locomotive to arrive a Dicot station was made by the Brown Boveri Company of Switzerland in 1955.

Steam Engine '1420' thought to be arriving at Radley station in 1950. The lamps on the front of the engine indicate that this was a Royal train, possibly on its way to Abingdon.

Lunchtime on 20 November 1955 was, to most people, a normal Sunday lunchtime. However, to the passengers of the 8.30a.m. Treherbert to Paddington excursion train it was a nightmare. The train was occupied, mostly, by members of the Womens Institute from the Welsh valleys. The crew consisted of engine driver Wheeler, aged fifty-five (with forty years service), and firemen Marsh, aged thirty (with thirteen and a half years' service) – both came from the Cardiff Canton shed. The guard was Mr Wall from Treherbert and the engine, a Britannia Pacific (No. 70026 *Polar Star*).

At approximately 1.10p.m. this giant engine and the first three coaches came crashing down the embankment between Milton and Didcot. The fourth and fifth coaches were torn apart as they came to a halt over all four tracks and the cafeteria coach crashed into the back of these and was severely damaged. Fortunately for some, the last four coaches remained undamaged. There were 293 passengers on the train; 11 were killed and 62 injured. The Ministry of Transport officer of inspection, Brigadier Langley, held driver Wheeler responsible for the crash. He honestly admitted that he did not see the signal when he ought to have done.

Mr Frank Dowding collects his medal and watch for twenty-five years of railway service.

In the shadows of *Cunnyngham Hall* in February 1965. Seen here are: George Price (traction inspector) Arthur Leaworthy (foreman), Harry Buckle (foreman) George East (shed master), Mr Loader (Divisional Manager), Mr Hanks (Divisional Traction Officer), Mrs Bray (clerk), Reg Warr (foreman), Ernie Jones (clerk), Mick Gleason, Vic Laity, Tom Edwards, Dave Aldridge, Jack Goodall, Eddie John, Arthur Wheatley, Charlie Taylor, Syd Hermon, Tony Young, George Wigley, Bob Looms, Ted Powell, Frank Downing, Ron Durman, Sam Morgan, Pat Walsh, Skip Morgan, Ted Brown, Mark Thomas, Jim Parsons, Charlie Skinner, Bill Warr, Ted Rock, Tom Smith, Lofty O'Connor, Dick Bidmean, Sid Davis, Jim Holmer, George Westall, E. Mole, Ernie Paul, Tony Neal, Pat Kelly, Cyril Dawson, Frank Marshall, Jim Tyler, Bill Cox.

Didcot railway workers at Kennington in 1970. Left to right: Phil Ireson, John Matherson, Des Sullivan, Les Stratton, Bob Johnson, Bob Howett, Roy Russell, Matt Oglesby.

Member so the Didcot staff club outing in 1963. Left to right, at the back: T. Edward, R. Lear, E. Paul. At the front: ? Rideout, Jack Butler (driver), V. Richard, J. Howard, D. Morrell, S. Lawrence, T. Neal.

A staff club outing in the 1960s. They include at the back: F. Feast, D. Morrell, T. Edward, P. Walsh. In the middle: ? Hughes, G. Bowen, V. Richards, Fay ?, B. Galloway, R. Lear, P. Northover, C. Thomas, C. Beck, C. 'Bronco' Ashmore, S. Lawrence, R. Butters. Sat at the front: A. Knapp, J. Cox, E. Paul, -?-, P. Rideout, B. Bennett.

The staff club on a coach trip to Southsea in the 1960s. Left to right, standing: D. Morrell, Jill May, C. Ashmore, H. Goodall, V. Richards, C. Thomas, -?-, Fay Bennett, G. Pratt, T. Edwards, Fay ?, -?-. Seated: T. Neal, Vic 'Ponty' Williams, P. Walsh. Enid Williams, -?-, Bill Pratt, E. Young, Brenda ?, E. Paul, M. Little.

The railway staff darts team, winners of the All Line Cup 1955/56/57/58. Left to right, back row: Les Stratton, Robert 'Mac' McConnell, Len Smith, Jimmy Austin. Front row: Morny Brown. Pete Aldridge, Frank Herman, Dick Greenaway.

A railway staff club dance. Left to right: Tom Tappin, Pam Smith, Pat Williams, Carmen Parsons, Ida Tappin, -?-, John Smith, Ted Williams, Cyril Parsons.

The staff of GWR's Didcot branch, staff winners of the Line Percussion Band contest. Among those seen here: Harold Coles, Mrs Pease, Beryl Haines, June Sugar, Yvonne Carter, Maurice Tugwell, Mrs Winkett.

In 1886 fire destroyed Didcot railway station. The photograph is reproduced by kind permission of Oxford County Council Photographic Archive.

Men survey the damage. The photograph is reproduced by kind permission of Oxford County Council Photographic Archive.

Six
The Military

The Didcot war memorial in Britwell Road. The Civic Centre is in the background.

LET the names of the Fallen be read that we may humbly
and gratefully remember them.

THE GREAT WAR 1914 – 1918

Douglas L Austin
Arthur Edwin Bennett
George Beck
Robert Bosher
William Bosley
Ernest Brind
William C. Brown
James Buller West
Joseph Davis
Hugh R. Dixon
A. John Eustace
Percival C. Fisher
James H. J. Forrest
Thomas Hartwell Coles

George W. C. Haycroft
Stanley A. Hillier
Albert Keats
Amos J. Keep
Arthur Keep
Walter F. Keep
Stanley B. Lewthwaite
Thomas Mooran
Albert F. Nobes
Sidney C. Nobes
John Norris
Victor Stimpson
Walter T. Stroud
William C. P. Wallace

WORLD WAR II 1939 – 1945

Harry Allen
Henry A. Allen
Ronald Arnold
Maurice Clifford Back
William G. Baker
Hubert D. Balsam
Fred Beaumont
John A. Beecham
Ernest G. Bowler
Ronald J. Brading
Charles Brogden
James Edward Brown
Clarence Victor Bull
Leslie George Bunting
Jack Carter
John Creed
Basil J. Chilver
Patrick L. Crabtree
Albert H. Didcock
Gordon H. Dixon
Rollo Dixon
Ernest Edwin Downing
John F. Dugan
Thomas James Evans
John Everitt
Arthur J. Frost
William Henry Gale
Oswald George
Frank Glover
Tony Goldring
H. V. (Vic) Goodall
Ronald P. Haynes

Albert Hall
Peter A. Hill
Albert R. Hooker
William A. Hughes
Vivion S. Hughes
Eric W. Leigh MM
Harry Eden Marriott
James Milne
Alan George Moore
Walter Edward John Noble
George Reeve
Anthony Roberts
Samuel Francis Roper
P. Jack Rouse
Phillip Ryding
Frederick J. Scrase
Eric Arthur Harry Shelley
Reginald J. Slade
Edward B. Soppet
Michael D. Stacey
Edgar R. Talbot
Joseph J. Taylor
Cyril Edward Town
George (Joey) Town
Reginald Welch
E. F. (Peter) Wells
Charles Wesson
Jack Weston
Basil Whitbread
Maurice J. Wigley
Aubrey Ralph Wilcher
Edward John Woodman

MAY GOD GRANT THEM ETERNAL REST

The plaque recording Didcot's fallen during the two wars.

A portrait of Alfred Burton (right) and a letter
(below), dating from 15 March 1944, that was
subsequently sent informing the family of Alfred
Burton (Oxford and Bucks Light Infantry and
Somerset Light Infantry) that he had been
wounded in action in Burma. Many people waited
with dread for similar letters from the War Office.

No. *Cao/13*
(If replying, please quote
above No.)

Army Form B. 104—81.

Infantry Record Office,

Exeter

15ᵗ March 19 *44*

~~Sir, or~~ MADAM,

I regret to have to inform you that a report has been received from
the War Office to the effect that (No.) *5353847* (Rank) *Private*
Name) *BURTON   Alfred William*
(Regiment) *Somerset Light Infantry* was wounded
on the *24ᵗ* day of *February* 19 *44*
in Burma. (gun shot wound shoulder) en

Amendment Slip to Army Form B:104—81.

It has not been reported into what hospital he has been
admi   admitted, nor are other particulars known, but in the event of his   ny
         condition being considered by the Medical Authorities as serious
furth   or dangerous this office will be notified by cable and you will be   ou.
         immediately informed   In addition he will have been given every
         facility for communicating with you himself.

I am to express to you the sympathy and regret of the Army
Council.

Mrs. W. Burton   Yours faithfully,

G.M. ....

Officer in charge of Records.

IMPORTANT.—Any change of address should be
immediately notified to this office.

(55827) M22108/1261 500m. P.&G. 9/39 52-4094   Form/B.104—81/4

A portrait of William Thompson, Royal Berkshires and Royal Engineers, from Bowness Avenue.

Malcolm Belcher who served with the Royal Engineers in Egypt and Italy.

Wally Nunn from the Royal Tank and
Parachute Regiment (RAOC), Dorsets.

Len and Wally Nunn. Len joined the Royal
Engineers at the early age of fifteen and
served with them for twenty-six years.

Joe Sear from the Tank Regiment, 8th Army.

Jim Smith, Oxford and Bucks Light Infantry.

Leonard Patrick Jennings.

William 'Bill' Ridley as a young soldier in the RAOC in 1927. These sort of stylized postcard were a feature of military life, particularly during the two world wars. Servicemen could send news and a picture of themselves back to their families.

115

Elsie Ridley, who served with the Indian Army is seen third from the right, back row, in 1944.

Vic Lyford in Italy with the Queen's Royal Regiment.

Cyril Parsons from the Royal
Engineers, seen in Africa.

John Keats, a Sergeant with REME.

On the left is Alf 'Darky' Keats who was a corporal with the DCLI. He is seen here at El Alemein in India with another unknown man.

The WREN, Muriel Winifred Gayley.

Left: Arthur Albert Gayley. *Right:* The wedding of Miss Dorothy Brown and Mr Les Longworthy DFC, RAF of Tavistock Avenue. Four months after this photograph was taken Les was reported killed in action after the Lancaster Bomber that he was in crashed over Germany on 10 January 1944. He was among a number of Vesta Estate boys that where killed in action. They included: Pat Crabree of Tavistock Avenue who served with the Royal Berks and died in France in 1944; Sam Roper of Tavistock Avenue who served with the Oxford and Berks and died in France in 1944; Jack Beaumont of Bowness Avenue who served with the Royal Tank Corps and died in Tobruk, Egypt, in 1942; John Creed of Bowness Avenue who served with the Royal Tank Corps and died in Tobruk, Egypt, in 1942; Jack Rouse from Parkside shop who served with RASC and died in the Middle East in 1942; James Evans from Bowness Avenue who served in the Navy and died in the Far East in 1942; Bob Hammond from Southpark Avenue who served with RASC and died in Italy in 1942.

Morny Brown from Tavistock Avenue who served with the Commandos in Burma.

Ted Brown seen when he was with the New Zealand Army. He came from Tavistock Avenue.

Jack Slade in Burma with the RAF.

Robert McConnell from the RAF.

Pte Eric S. Fisher from the RASC.

The Wheatsheaf public house during the war. Standing at the back is Young Ted Turner. Left to right, sitting at the front: Jim Turner, Joe Turner (father of Ted), Ted Turner, Jobie Lloyd.

Sergeant Charles Henry Caulkett, father of the author, who served for twenty-three years in the army. Nine of these years were seen with the Ninth Lancers and fourteen were spent with the Royal Army Veterinary Corps. He was a veteran of Dunkirk and saw service in Ireland, Egypt, Palestine, France and took part in the battle of Monte Casino.

Les Rees from South Park Avenue, who served with the Navy in HMS *Mermaid* and HMS *Comus*.

Ted Turner who worked on Fleet Air arm landing crafts aboard HMS Burwell.

Comrades on Bowness Avenue. Left to right they are: Brian Abbot (RAF), Gwilyn Evans from South Park Avenue (Royal Navy), Geoff Mellotie.

Left to right: Fred Sear who served on HMS *Faulkener* during the First World War, Bert Sear who was a shunter at Didcot Depot, -?-.

On the left is Gwilym Evans from South Park Avenue who served on HMS *Sirius*. In the middle is Dicky Reece from Parkside who served on the aircraft carrier *Formidable*. To the right is Neil Williams from South Park Avenue who was a commando with the Royal Navy.

Left to right: Bob Willis, Bob Gosford, Arthur Bennett.

The wedding of Walter Leonard Smith from Tavistock Avenue (chief stoker on one of the mine sweepers) and Elizabeth Best in 1936. Elizabeth's father and grandfather were riggers and both served in the Royal Navy.

James Evans from South Park Avenue (top left) with shipmates from HMS *Danae*. James was listed as missing in action in the Far East in 1942. James' brother Gwilym never found out what happened to James but it is widely believed that he was taken off ship to work a steam locomotive. The War Office could not come up with an appropriate answer.